The Amerikkk

The Amerikkkan Nightmare

A collection of poems

Written by Amber Hasan and Zaahid Hasan

The Hasan Group and Weird Doze LLC.

In collaboration with Eye of the Storm Publishing

St. Louis, Mo.
Atlanta, Ga.
Eye of the Storm Publishing
Atlanta, Ga.

The Hasan Group
Michigan

Weird Doze LLC.
St. Louis, Mo.

ISBN: 978-0-578-90539-6

Dedicated to:

Allah (SWT)

And

The ancestors who conspired together to ensure our survival

Forward

My brother and I began this process while I was on bed rest after tearing my Achilles tendon, and then being diagnosed with Lupus. My brother, Zaahid, was incarcerated at the time when this project started. This work began as a series of letters that we would write to each other in poetic format. We were both being faced with our human weaknesses and the letters were a way for us both to maintain some peace within our personal chaos, we used our words and our love for each other as siblings to fuel our dedication to self-preservation. That dedication to self-preservation that black people have has always been The Amerikkkan Nightmare. It was such a gift to be able to share this time of struggle and perseverance with my brother, who was also dealing with his own battles. This book is a tribute to our ancestors, a gift of gratitude to honor their legacy. After nine years of reworking the material we are at a place where we are pleased with our work, and we thank the Creator of All things for giving us the opportunity to share our journey and art with the world.

With gratitude,
- Amber Hasan

Table of Contents

Afraid of my Dreams

This is my apology
To everybody I did wrong,
And everybody I stepped on
The truth is I was dead wrong,

Robbed girls of their innocence,
swindled out of virginities

They thought I was super-man,
But they were sleeping with the enemy

That's just what it is

Life is such a bitch,
justice went to jail
and the devil was the snitch

This world I live in,
Seems like everything is switched,
I like the Cinderella's but I love the
wicked witch

Got no grasp of reality, no sense of sanity
A victim and a witness of classic human
conditioning

...Been working on myself

But I notice when things get better, Mother
Nature interferes and then she changes the
weather

Life happens in seasons,
Been living without a reason,
Still breathing without a purpose,
know how it feels to be worthless?

I been close to the edge, but I'll never go over that
On the brink of success, I woke up and I noticed that
I never get to slow up,
Wishing that my parents never broke up,
Had me choked up,
And lately I've been dealing with some more stuff
But you know what…

Maybe that's the reason I tend to blow up

Almost dropped out during High-School, because I never wanted to show up
And I ask how
been locked-up half of my adult life now,
The loudest is the weakest in the room, and I can't pipe down
Keep climbing up the ladder to the top and then I slide down
I didn't care at first
But it has me asking why now

Smoking weed, trying to take the pain away
Got used to the weather,
looking forward to the rainy days
Took so many Xanax, I tried to self prescribe and medicate,
Drinking liquor everyday,
Scared to be sober,
On my way to hell,
I bet Granny is turning over,
I wonder what my son will think of me when he gets older

And everything is everything

But life ain't what it seems,
Don't want to go to sleep no more
I'm afraid of my dreams

"As I lay me down to sleep,
I keep having these visions of taking care of business
And dreams that I keep winning"

But whenever I'm woke,
I notice I'm broke
Life robbed me of my innocence and robbed me of my hope

So I stay sleeping

Things keep changing
Time keeps creeping
Nightmares become welcome signs
More benign than deferred dreams
Lines blurred as the birds sing

Signaling morning

But I can't grieve what I won't let die
Eyes closed
Mind froze
How will I ever see beyond the sky
Beyond my failures
Beyond my lies
Can't cultivate truth if I don't even try
It's often easier to lay in wait
In state of paralysis
Boo Hag riding me
Which way do I go
Am I the only one who feels stuck and doesn't know

Or is everyone just wandering
Wondering
Wanting
Waiting
Contemplating
Praying for peace from the most Supreme

Barely staying afloat
Hardly staying awoke
Because I’m afraid of my dreams

To Infinity and Beyond

Inching towards infinity
While trying to gain the ability to
understand that this too will come to an end

All burdens
All blessings
All foes
All friends

All blend together with beautiful
brushstrokes
Designing the dimensions of who I've been

Will become

Connecting where I'm headed with where I'm
from

The clock keeps ticking
I think it's getting louder
Chronomentrophobia sets in
I may be suffering from a captain hook
complex
But I don't think Neverland is an option
The coffin gets closer by the second
Heaven or hell could be a heartbeat away
That day will surely arrive
Already been scribed
Can't bribe the reaper
No price is steeper than that

Nothing deeper than the fact that
we are all inching towards infinity
While trying to figure out
how to let go of the finite things

Or bring ourselves to see that even though forever exists
Doesn't mean that we will exist in it

Can't fight kismet
Or the law of Physics
Energy only changes,
never ceasing its existence
Oceans that are endless
That reach into the abyss
Waiting to be explored, make this discovery your Plymouth

But just because you found it
Doesn't make you the founder
Somebody was there before you,
that's the nature of this cycle
Certain circles believe in death being a weakness,
Something we can cure as if it can be defeated
Searching for fountains of youth
Instead of mountains of truth

I'm sure that's the same fruit that Eve started to chew

So I guess its human nature
to ask the question why
I was told from the beginning
life is hard and then you die
Only legacies last forever,
and the stories of endeavors
In the end those trying to be God
Tend to look just like the devil…

Cobain

It’s heavenly

Somewhere in the vicinity of Nirvana

Drama doesn’t exist here

Just mirrors

Reflectors

Self checkers

Protectors of the truth

Group therapy for loners, which is what we all are

Not ashamed of my scars

Far from perfect

But close to the creator

I think I’ve found my chi

Be boldly, unapologetically human young grasshopper

We build up all this anxiety trying to please society

Dreaming up polite ways to be imperfect

Trying not to ripple the surface

Trying to trick the serpent

into thinking that we have a working

knowledge of our power

trying to hide our inner coward

we end up spending most of our energy

dodging the final hour

to no avail

got to fail sometimes

live life in Braille sometimes

feeling your way through the rough spots

its dark and hell is hot, or so I hear

when it's unclear just play it by ear

listen to your inner critic

kill your inner cynic

replace limits with goals, embrace yourself

whole

know when to fold and when to walk away

everyday is a gamble, an audition for your

mission

the truest gifts of existence are wrapped in

second chances and forgiveness

that's what living has taught me

the pain that heartbreak has brought me is a

constant reminder

to be kinder

originality is just a speech class for the

mimer

make ever move timeless, forget about the

timer

be proud enough to be a pawn

humble enough to be the king

on a hobbit has what it takes

to be the lord of the ring

decrease to the size of a baby

in order for the creator to increase into

something major,

your role might be to tow for the rest of

those on the boat

who figured that the greatest of all would

be the goat

watching for the isolated monsters inside

the moat

optical illusion is the best defense for

intrusion

make them focus on the beauty, confuse it

with the truth

mystification is just intimidation

the fear of the unknown leaves growth

stagnated

propagandous manipulation

certain things always remain changeless

who lied and said there's a thin line

between love and hatred

confuse the basic principles of a power that

sacred

then feed it to the flow and watch them take

it

forget the battle you're fighting

no hope in winning the war

we say "in God we trust"

then proceed to lock our doors

it seems we forget to pray, until it's time

to crash

only in the aftermath do we notice the faith

we lack

surely if I could move mountains with a

mustard seed

I should be able to move molehills with what

I have currently,

Heat check

Just to see that I'm lukewarm

For too long,

Gotta stop it

just my moral compass

No peripheral view available when wearing

blinders

Beware of newcomers

Take heed to the old-timers

Leave mistakes behind

And bury all the particulars

And make sure your path to the top remains

perpendicular

Untitled 2

I'm creeping,
Thinking of leaping
Don't need any assistance,
too close to the ledge for resistance
Tempted to take the dive
But there is a mustard seed on the other side of the scales

Opposite the weight of the world

I pray that is enough to keep me balanced
because when all hope has vanished
Faith is all I have
It's like a jungle sometimes;
it makes me wonder why I'm still fighting

Still writing my way past my woes

Being closed is the only way to avoid clicking
Time bomb ticking inside my hurt locker
Waiting to be disarmed
I keep my distance
so innocent victims wont be harmed
Because even the fragments from someone else's pain
Can leave your heart paralyzed or slain
The rain falls on the just and the unjust

I'm just existing right now

It's all I can do to keep from dying
I'd be lying if I said I wasn't just lingering
Trying to find something solid to hold on to
Something meaningful to get into
Some surface to scratch
in order to hatch some of these dreams

I'm fiending for some substance
    craving solace

Seems like I've been here before

Like a reoccurring theme

Talking without a purpose
And listening to a whole lot of nothing

My conscious strikes me in the face
No time to waste
So I think of a plan,
and that's where I drift away

I realized I'd rather live atop the clouds
I guess the true gift of the high is feeling closer to God,

Overactive imagination and an underactive follow thru
Trife is a life of dormancy,
Life continues
But the only thing that seems to remain the same
is my stagnancy

The author of my own life,
cursed with writers block
Dictator of my destiny
But resting and wrestling
With these thoughts going 100 different ways
in the corridors of my mind
Leaving me so confined

Eyes open,
Gawking
Inattentive when I'm walking

Could say that I'm on track but the train is headed for me
Can't see,
started in a tunnel of darkness
Then a light
And an engine
And the smoke
Then the fright
Of a freight
headed quickly my way
What a sight
What to do?
My feet keep carrying me that way
Without a blueprint from my brain
Feeling hopeless,
feeling helpless
Feeling insane

Looking death right in the eye,
thinking pain
A light flashes when the train gets 2 inches away
That's when I wake up and get started with my day
jumping quickly out of bed
aggressively grabbing life by the neck
because the only thing that comes to a sleeper is a dream
so I gotta get up
start to fill up my cup
instead of knocking on the door
self-instruction or self-destruction
cause
no
instructions
come
with
this
weapon

that
I'm
Carrying

I don't want the radio edit version of being a person
I want the whole experience, blame my indulgent nature
It keeps me on pins and needles
In search of satisfying stimulation
My idle mind is a minefield
Littered with orchids and daisy's
Trees ripe with pink ladies
And this is where I vacation
Where I feel closest to the vibration of creation
All insecurities are latent
My internal security blanket
Always on the brink of a breakthrough or a breakdown
Sometimes I break out in song or scripture
I hum melodies to memories
And become enslaved by my soliloquies
I'm simply surviving right now
This is an idiots guide to perseverance
An ode to the spirit
A users guide to being fearless

Waiting For My Death

You know rain makes the flowers grow, but be careful what you're wishing for.

Every rose has its thorns

I fell in love with the silence that precedes the storm
And fell in hate with the noise of sounding the alarm

Ever took a second to reckon why clowns paint frowns?

The smell of death is the reason the vultures come around, see that raven perched high, that black dog in the shadows… Even the rats of the sewer see the maggots of the future…

The latter is exactly why I walk under the ladder
Step on every crack
And punch the mirror til it shatters
Take a piss on fields of flowers
Defecate into the dirt
We fertilize the mind with shit in hopes that something else will grow
When it's been proven true that you reap the fruit you grow…

Lurking in the wait, I feel the stares of fixation
Waiting for the bad news, tell them to be patient

Hyenas sit in disguise laughing loud at every blunder
What do they profit or make from the meat of my mistakes?
When my heart was filled with life all were absent at the time
But they all seem numerous at my funeral
Downfall
Of a downcast
Downtrodden
Down nigga
I guarantee they download that in their downtime
CTRL+ALT+DELETE
Being a sheep will get you slaughtered
Martyred like Mufasa
King of the jungle,
caged by civilization
Seen as a danger but too low on the food chain to change
They say its human nature
Only the strong survive genocide,
evolution by elimination
By sterilization
By stagnation
So I got to keep pacing
Run this race like the tortoise
See the forest,
the trees,
the grass,
the leaves
Enjoy every breeze
Breathe before I speak
Look before I leap
Be true to myself so that I can sleep at night
Even when I'm wrong always believe in right
Wish blessing on those who detest me
Even those who desire my eternal resting

Even if the final plot is to nail me to the cross
As they nail me ask God to forgive them for their faults, as their waiting on my death

The Amerikkkan Nightmare

People do the worst things
in the name of Glory, God, and Gold
We turn into captors and conquerors
Sponsors of inequity
Killers of any dream
Sellers of anything, buyers of facades
They make struggling taboo now people scared
to say Jihad
But it's cool if you say "nigga"
Or sit at home without a job
And yes the media's behind it
that's their cotton-picking job
Take cotton-picking descendants
Make em happy to be niggas
No conspiracy or rumor, we are the American
tumor
So the only good nigga is either dead or a
consumer
Buried in debt
Check to check stressin'
Blood pressure up popping pills for
depression
It's hard to worry about drones
and clones,
governments tapping our phones
When you're one payment away from losing
your home
You're not truly a homeowner if you took out
a loan,
and that's real
The banks name is on the plot
we're just tending the fields
For 30 years plus interest
Better watch these Brooks Brothers henchmen,
Their just pimpin' in a better wardrobe
Playing monopoly with your homes

They make "no fly" zones in other peoples country,
Then build a fence around their own
They steal elections and arm insurrections
The only complexion that matters is green
Capitalism. Rules. Everything. Around. Me
But CREAM always rises to the top
Transcendentalist thoughts of their transmogrific plots
Take the scholars of Harlem, in essence the black Harvard
Turn em into crack lovers and just watch em kill each other
Forecast reads downfall
Drown yall with sugar water & Alcohol
Let em have basketball
But don't let them get too involved
That way they can de-evolve,
Now notice
The monkeys on your back for the long haul
They lock us in prison then charge an arm for a phone call
I bet it didn't cost this much for E.T. to phone home
Thought of being a doctor or scientist are now long gone
So we've fallen
We're falling
We fell right into the snare
Burlesque dialogue makes you think they really care
Bonafide austerity, cant you feel it in the air?
Blow up a whole village just to take its oil fields
Sometimes fortune is unfortunate,
a chain can get you killed
So now more than ever we need that providential healing

Praying to the God above for divine
intervention
From this place that speaks loud,
but doesn't look, learn or listen
We're being put in a position for inevitable
submission
Check mate in 3 moves, don't let the smooth
taste fool ya
Step 1 to liberation don't let ego rule ya
Step 2 if all else fails never forget Step 1
And learn when to surrender
When to fight
And when to run!

Super Saiyan

Bottled water brain,

Purified thoughts

Translucent dreams

Bright black realities

Snow white lies I ignored…

Kept peace

Repent in this realm just to save face

Undisturbed lake, visible bottom

The usual dark tunnel kept the light on today

Freshly bloomed flowers, reminiscent of summer

Naked personality without the eyes of consciousness

No watchers

Just me and my craft,

First I slowly caress it

Kiss it from head to toe

Then I release the beast and we become one

My body suddenly becomes my body of work,

The basket grows wider

Seemingly I can't miss,

The uprights spread apart creating infinite

ease

Incredible impulse,

Futuristic vision

Natural reactions are the best choice

No fear

I can dive off this building

and guarantee a perfect 10 on my landing

Into a glass of water

Defeating all impossibilities

My prayers and meditations become beautiful

symphonies

To infinity and beyond

Bathing in bronze tinted breezes,

warm moments of existence leave us longing

for longevity

Making the brevity of everything amplified

Sound waves crashing

Scored by the everlasting

Ever evolving

Emotional being

Self-acceptance is freeing

Conspicuous consumer of positive vibes

From a tribe of happy hybrids

Lavish

Explosive

Vibrant

A verb personified

Bird like

Flight taken

The earth's energy erupting internally

Eternal inferno

Great balls of fire

Juggling anger and desire

Channeling the spirit of Goku

"I am the hope of the universe"

Oxymoron

warrior dedicated to upholding peace

becoming complete

an epiphany caused great relief

"completeness will always

and forever be slightly beyond reach"

3 Wise Men

What is the worth of wisdom, knowledge and understanding?

To capture it in it's essence?

Not the way the world dresses it

Solomonic intelligence reserved for the majestic

Or the attitude learned from the trials of a peasant.

So bleak is the eye that perceives the meek as weak

The humility it takes for the king to wash your feet

Arcane is the origin of this crudité lore,

what you didn't need before

you taste it once and need more,

but only if this world had 3 wise men,

the 1-eyed ruler wouldn't lead the blind then

walk us all off of a cliff

and hustle different dreams to buy,

I guess we'll all dwell in the dark

until we learn to open eyes,

Open books and open hearts

Open up and open minds

Use logical reasoning versus cultural

seasoning

Everything has a season

Even a so-called heathen has something they

believe in,

Something they would die for

A reason why they live

A universal truth hid behind dogma

Reality is relative,

that's the drama of existence

Our flaws and our forgiveness solidifies our

kinship

All creation connected

The wise man knows to be careful when

choosing weapons

Because they can easily become the tools

of your own oppression

But wisdom like reality only lives in theory

Sounds better on paper

Ignorance is safer

The scapegoat of the sheep,

Crutch of the weak

Living to avoid the agony of defeat

Weep for those who believe their own hype

Can't write your own eulogy

Just love solemnly and live truthfully

Isn't that wisdom after all?

Aware enough to recognize you'll never

understand it all

Truth is if we were all able to comprehend

The value would surely shrink,

and it wouldn't be worth a cent

That makes to worth of wisdom infinitely

endless

Infinite and endless

Infinite or endless?

Which causes us to see

that at least 1 wise man can be the change

the world needs…

Pi

I feel good even when I'm bad

feeling up even when I'm down

I wanna frown but I force a smile

I didn't even complain about having to run this mile
I went from run this town to having to run from this town
I fit in even outta town
even overseas I made friends not enemies

made love, not war or strife
made life, not death or fights

I feel confident with the world against me, managed to fuck it all up when the world was with me

was banking on the wrong things
the sex, the lies, the dreams, clothes, cars, and the bling
even when I'm all out I still give my all

I'm the new caged bird, come and hear my song

up beat even when I'm beat up
they give me the middle finger,

I throw the peace up

The only G up is God

no sob stories
only the glory of growth

taking oaths to myself to be better with
every beat

3.1415926535

irrationally incomplete

Infinite possibilities for mishaps and
atonement

no need to squeeze the power from every
moment
some seconds should be reserved for still

distilled

connoisseured

savored

save some of its memory for the
descendants to dine on
maybe they will meet the manifestation of my
mistakes

sew the talents I left planted and harvest
something great

so that I can be present even when I'm
absent
be alive even when I die
stay active in my placidity
be happy even when I cry

Open Windows Close Fast

When your number is called be sure to answer
keep the phone close
and ringer turned up before the forest burns
up
cant put out that inferno once it starts
blazing
the picture was drawn in pen, enemy of the
eraser
the second that the window is ajar better
climb through it
can't break it once it's closed
for insurance they bulletproofed it,
armor guarded it for extra measure
there's hidden treasure on the other side,
but only a few seconds is it open wide
better step through the door while it's open
because the moment they push it shut,
time is up
and don't nobody give a fuck
you missed the train and there is no
rescheduling
no more entry into the society
of once-in-a-lifetime opportunity
doesn't matter if you have a passport
and speak the language fluently
what is meant for you won't miss you
so let the windows close without scrutiny
dwelling in the realm of "what if" can cause
lunacy
when no exit route exists inward is the only
escape route
excavate your caves, might be gold in those
hills
mines in this mind
solace for suffering
sight for blind
release from binds

which I only find when I become fine in my confined spaces
windows don't matter when I don't need to leave here
I am spacious
I am open
I am patient
I am oasis

Achilles, Heal

We all have a breaking point

No matter how many myths they create about
our greatness we all have a tender tendon
that tells the truth about our mortality

Exposes our humanity

Breaks us down to the dust particles
that we were created from

Forced to face our flagrant frailty

We lay in wait

Shaped by fate
held together by faith

Our only recourse is to make the best of it
Make lemonade
Make memories
Make tomorrow better than today
Play and pray

Color in the grey areas with your favorite
shades
Even if that means florescent beige
Earth tones can be iridescent on the darkest
days,
and that can be enough to illuminate the
maze

The labyrinth of living
No thread of Ariadne giving us a way out
No Minotaur to defeat

Our purpose is to ascend and transcend

without having to depend or defend

Made of earth,
fire,
wind,
water,
sound waves,
light rays

Sugar & Spice

Blood & Bread

And Melanin.

Constantly aware of the settlers
settling on discovering what has always
been.

Inherently owned by the indigenous
from whom good will was granted.

Good seeds were planted.

Taking care of the planet was never taken
for granted.

And since, we've been mishandled.

What was once firm
has been masterfully uprooted and looted.

Diagnosis of systemic abuses, they call us
stupid.

The same entity set us up and used us,
then called us useless.

Commanding, "Lift yourself by your bootstraps"
to the shoeless.

Adding more fuel to the fire,
more weight to the bar,
more stress to the situation.

Til then I am sturdying my sturdiest structures
and reinforcing what had yet to pressured,
prolonging the second
That moment that we all fear,
but a moment that must come none the same.

We all have a breaking point.

In the clouds somewhere

Where the smoke and the fog become one

Frogs come expecting kisses from Princes

Mental fences get scaled

And prison shackles dematerialize before the eyes

Before the laughs and the cries: the claps and the sigs

Be grateful that I allow you to take this ride to the other side of existence

Buckle up but don't check the rear view

There is no hope for a clear view

Let your minds eye steer you

A sort of compass to the unseen

A guide to doing the undone

But what hasn't been done under the sun

Under duress

Under stress

Under paid

What no one understands is that most days I

just want to crawl up under a rock

Instead I float to where the fog meets the

smoke

Where my dreams encounter hope with a

handshake

Trying to find balance between doing stuff

for mankind   or for mans sake

I’m a Samurai on his lunch break

Drinking coffee spiked with sake

Too much on my dinner plate

So I break fast with a glass of water

Neither half empty nor half full

I push and pull trying find my equilibrium

Exchanging greetings with the ancestors

The ocean told me even when I’m crashing

I should keep flowing

The sun woke me up and said,
“shine so bright that they have to create
new terms to define your glow”

the birds told me to be heard and be ready
to move, got to be early to get the seeds

The wind sang, harmonizing with the trees

The rain and the waves gave me rhythm and
reason

Say:
Dance wherever your are,
talk in feet, and arms, and hips
You are well equipped
Toolbox full,
but a hammer can't build a home on it's own
Needs a hand to swing it,
energy to bring it to final formation

Which is forever changing and hard to grasp
like how the greatest threat to mankind is
the mosquito

Hard to understand
like taking a Camel through the eye of a
needle

Hard to control
like a Billy goat's libido

Hard to explain
like why we all want to be regal,
can't rule another human when I haven't
mastered myself
and queens kiss toads
then the fog explodes into the sunshine

In a world full of 8 billion people I just
need some
1 on 1 time
Some numb time

Flight of the bumblebee
Catch my own beat
Drum line
Cannon to the right of them
Cannon to the left of them
At war with me, myself, and I
trying to liberate the best of them
Even in the smoke and fog of my darkest days
it’s always too late to question fate
So I soldier on
no such thing as mistakes
The decisions are made
each step a march to my grave
In the charge of the light brigade

Untitled (The American Nightmare)

People do the worst things in the
names of Glory, God, or Gold
We turn into captors & conqueres
Sponsors of inequity
Killers of any dream
sellers of anything
buyers of facades
they make struggling taboo
Now ppl scared to say Jihad
But it's cool if you say nigga
sit at home w/out a job
and yeah the medias behind it
thats their cottonpickin job
take cottonpickin decendents
make em happy to be niggas
No conspiracy or rumor
we are the American Tumor
the only good nigga
is either dead or a consumer
buried in debt
check to check
Stressin
blood pressure up
popping pills for depression

Original Copy of "Amerikkkan Nightmare"

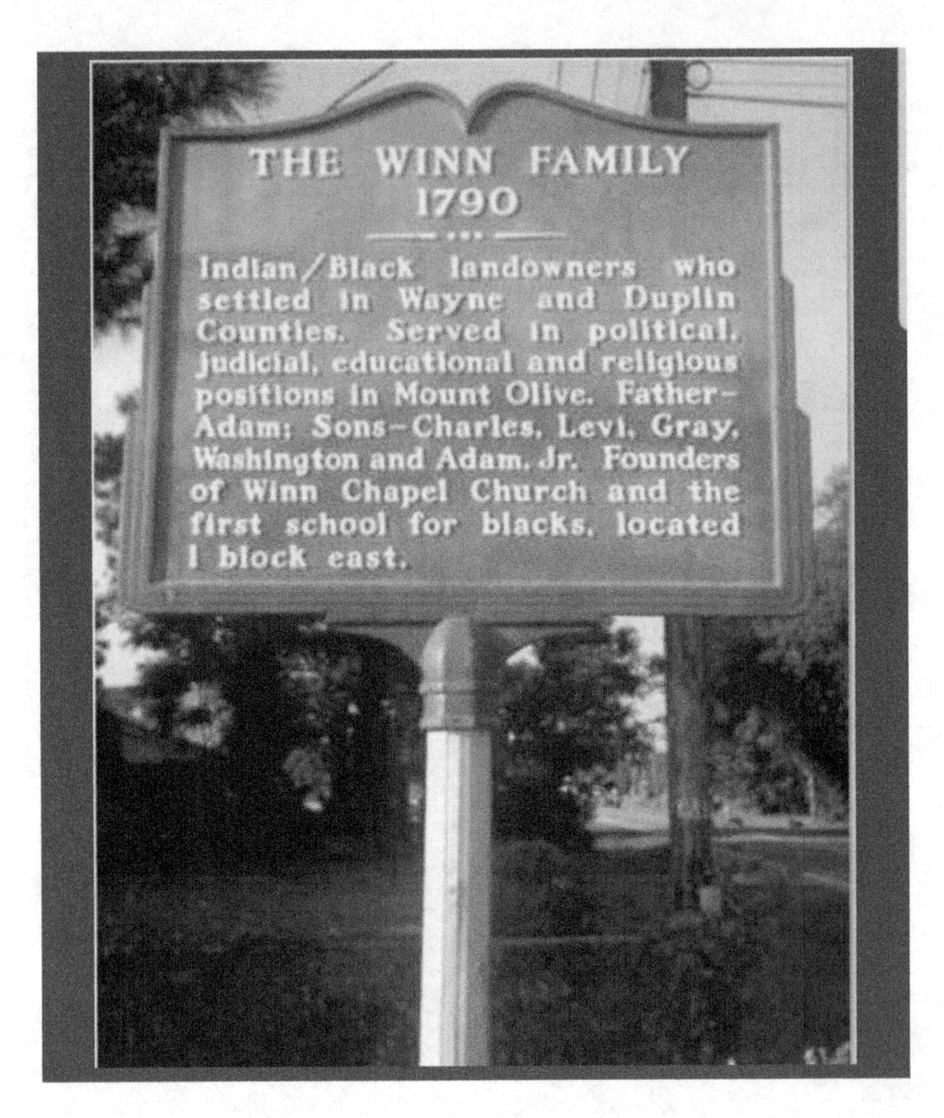

Ancestral Plaque honoring our 4th and 5th Maternal Great Grandfathers Levi and his father Adam Winn who were free black North Carolinians (Wayne Count, N.C.)

<of note: one resource mentions that King George III issued over 200 acres of land in Duplin County to Adam Winn Sr. >

In the 1850 census, the Winn Family is listed as "mulatto", but in the 1860 census, they were listed as "black".

<of note: one resource mentions that the Winns were originally Waccamaw Indians and many of their descendents were from "Sir Walter Raleigh's Lost Colony" and were never slaves; always FREE men; no record that they ever purchased freedom>

The Winn Family were FREE blacks, from Duplin County, who had received their freedom prior to 1834. The Artis, Simmons, and Greenfield families of Mount Olive were also free blacks, according to the 1860 census.

Information retrieved from Ancestry.com about our 5th Maternal Great Grandfather Adam Winn Sr. (Adam was free, but was also a slave owner)

Maternal Grandmother, Carrie Bates, (unknown male) Maternal Great Grandmother Annie Rawson (Rowson/Rausom) (Right)

Paternal Great Grandfather (Charles Quitman Moore),2nd Great Aunt (Ida Moore), 2nd Great Grand parents, (Martha "Mattie" Moore (Nelson) and Otho Moore), and 2nd Great uncle (Tandy Moore)

Family praying after the passing of Paternal Great Aunt "Babe" Fannie Moore, (Adopted Grandmother)

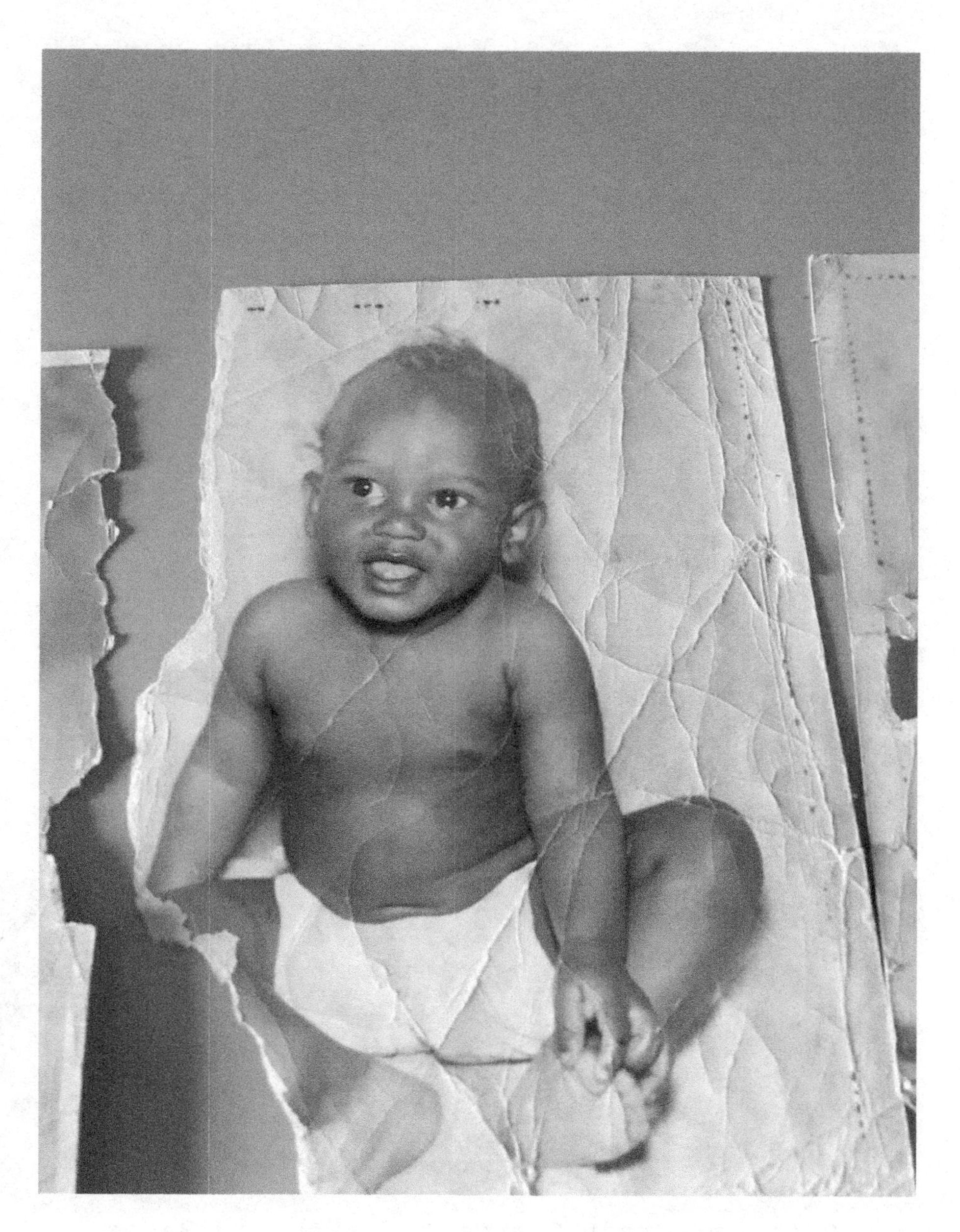

Father Tyrone Ward Sr.

Maternal Great Grandfather Raymond Bates

Paternal 2nd Great Grandmother Elizabeth "Lizzie" Ward

Maternal grandfather, Melvin "Dickie" Bates

Paternal Grandmother Lorene (Denham) Ward

Paternal Grandfather Oliser Ward Sr.

Paternal 3rd Great Grandmother Martha Ann Curtis McGough

Paternal Great Uncle Fred Moore (Adopted Grandfather)

Mother Lynette Ward

Original letters from the planning of the book November 2012.

*** In this book we paid homage to some of our ancestors through photographs. These only represent the ancestors who we have photographs of, but in no way diminishes the impact and influence that those who are not pictured had on our existence. Those unnamed are just as important as those who are named. We are currently researching our family genealogy and have found out some amazing information. We encourage all people, but especially African Americans and those of the African Diaspora to research their family history. The things that we learn from our past can help us to create a better future.

Made in the USA
Monee, IL
08 November 2023